Top Teen Greatest Hits

Top Teen Greatest Hits

poems by

Carol Wierzbicki

POETS WEAR PRADA • Hoboken, New Jersey

Top Teen Greatest Hits

Poets Wear Prada
533 Bloomfield Street, Second Floor
Hoboken, New Jersey 07030
http://pwpbooks.blogspot.com

First North American Publication 2009
Second / Mass Market Paperback Edition 2017

Grateful acknowledgment is made to the following publications where some of these poems have previously appeared:

Dreamscapes, Evergreen Review, Long Shot, The Outlaw Bible of American Poetry (Thunder's Mouth Press), and *The Unbearables Assembling Magazine.*

ISBN-13: 978-0-9817678-7-1
ISBN-10: 0-9817678-7-7

Printed in America

Front & back cover design: Electrofork
Author's Photo: Pieter van Hattem

For me, adolescence was the regrettable passage from childhood to the demands of hormones and higher education. For Carol Wierzbicki, it became the *Top Teen Greatest Hits*. . . . She writes as if she were an observer during her rite of passage, even stepping back when she was five and six, taking in situations and translating growing pains into mini stories. Mundane occurrences, whether sad or funny, are refreshing to read, filled with insight and lessons.

— Gently Read Literature

Her metaphor of ashes [in "Karl, Esther, Mark"] makes it one of the most powerful pieces . . . while maintaining the facade of nothing serious. She connects scenes through their connections to ash and grieves over them strangely: "Now I'm the nomad on horseback, / scattering Karl and Esther's ashes over London: / they dribble from the end of my / neglected cigarette."

— The Hudson Reporter

Carol autographed my copy with a note: "I can't think of anything clever to write." Not true! Right in the first poem, she writes: "A bomb explodes around me; / I am its center." In a bittersweet series of 14 glances back at youth, she manages to capture regret, amusement, curiosity, bafflement, longing, nostalgia: "I wonder these days where those skateboard boys / of my neighborhood ended up: / . . . [with] their defiant crew cuts / . . . / whispering plans in the trenches." Yes!

— Bart Plantenga, author of *Paris Scratch*

Top Teen Greatest Hits

For Paul, who helped me through adolescence by being my brother

Contents

Adolescence

Sparks fly —
I rub the cat backwards.
He screams, then bolts like a horse
Out the closet door.

A bomb explodes around me;
I am its center.

In the middle of a tornado
There is no wind
(Gray stallions leap and plunge around).

The wheat is in danger. But I am calm
Or try to be
While I stay locked in this house
And locusts hum and chew.

Firecracker Wedding Poem
for Cliff & Megan

Firecracker, bottle rocket, M-80 —
the words whiz past my head
as boys kneel on sidewalks
making fires for their gods
and are frozen in a moment of wonder
as they watch the
glittering gold ejaculate
stream down to earth.

My brother for a brief phase
in his life lit bombs:
smoke, cherry, stink.
But after the many false starts of his adolescence
he fell, diffused, into
troubled adult silence. I hope he finds his way
back to the light.

The Roman candles, the pinwheels —
I wanted them at my wedding,
but the small backyard could hold only
food, drink and family, not light or raucous blasts.

I wonder these days where those skateboard boys
of my neighborhood ended up:
I can still see them, their defiant crew cuts
shining spiky in the sun like new-mown hayfields,
and at dusk,
sending off chute after chute of liquid gold,
scrambling about,
whispering plans in the trenches,
trying to keep back the dark.

To a Young Swimmer

You could beat me in a race
if you weren't afraid to
come into the deep end.
It's disorienting at first,
the tortoiseshell patterns made by the light
on all sides,
not just the pool floor.

You slip weightless through the ether
but are tethered by fear.
I want to press on though
gravity's closing in.

See that stand of trees?
Beyond them lies the scorched earth
of my adolescence.
I tried to drown my insecurities
in chlorinated silence,
hold my awkwardness under
till it turned blue.

I want to coax you out
but I see you are untroubled
by your limitations,
content to stay in the shallow end,
your loud pink sex toys bobbing
at the edge.

By the time I was your age
I was already swimming at all depths,
pushed by a need
I am still trying to define.

Ice Skating

I'm 16 and skating
around and around the ring,
trying to make sense of how
life's treated me so far.

In the center, doing lopsided spins,
I'm like the dog circling and circling nose to tail,
trampling reality to make his bed of comfort
dizzying the world to a blur
before it can shake me apart.

Suddenly ELO's "Livin' Thing" comes on over the
    loudspeakers
and it all clicks. I head out to the far edge,
hugging the wall for maximum speed,
the gypsy violins squeezing out my hurt
and replacing it with adrenaline.

The ice is forgiving.
It cradles my blades.
My stride is sure
from hip to toes.

Session's ending. The vapid cha-cha version of
"What Now My Love" blasts
behind the announcer's voice.
As the ice empties I sneak one last victory lap
as if my life depended on it
and for now, it does.

Driver's Ed

Suddenly I'm piloting
a two-ton metal fat suit.
Boys who didn't pass Freshman Math
turn the wheel with one hand.
Everything is ass-backwards;
my skills mean nothing here.
Spatial perception is
not intuitive,
and I've missed the class on passing
and use of the rear-view mirror.
The gym teacher who doubles
as our class instructor
believes in teaching by humiliation:
"*Bam!* You just ran into him! Where's your blind spot?"
I sure know where yours is, I retort, and for my impertinence
he assigns me writing out the 12 rules of passing
ten times for homework.
I type it, then hand it in.
My brand of dexterity, at least, counts for something.

Collecting Butterflies

Mother thought my brother's hobby a gentle one —
the caught butterfly or moth was
chloroformed in the relaxing tray,
thus spared a more violent death.
But I saw something disturbingly
inscrutable and profound
in the pansy-like faces,
the beady eyes and furry, pollen-seeking tongues,
and the gossamer green net sailing through the air
reminded me of the one in cartoons
used to bag insane escapees.

Wasn't it we the collectors
who suffered from temporary madness
induced by the beauty of those powdered wings?
The majesty of the Polyphemus moth
whose blue-and-brown wings
and leonine face
embodied the nighttime ramblings
of our minds?

My family visited the Cranbrook Institute of Science often;
now, those were pristine picklings —
the bodies had been replaced entirely
with trompe l'oeil
pieces of cardboard;
the giant African wings
shone with a reproachful blue-green sheen.
I thought of the disheveled bodies at home
smashed in cellophane:
how could I know that those amateur embalmings
would become powder —
fossilized by Paul's sudden indifference?

Getting His Shoes Shined in Nassau

"Shoeshine for $1!"
Inexplicably, my brother Paul decides to do it,
goes over to the 12-year-old
who shouted it.
My mother, father, and I watch
as Paul places one of his
Brady Bunch brown boots
on the box.
The cloth goes back and forth
vigorously over the leather;
it's a blur.
The kid stops, rests on his heels
then *Bonk! Bonk!*
he knocks the handle of his brush
on the box.
Stares at Paul.
Bonk! Bonk! again.
Paul takes a guess and
shifts feet.
The cloth blurs.
Bonk! Bonk!
Paul hesitates, then shifts feet.
Bonk! Bonk! the kid flips the brush
in the air,
knocking it and tossing it in one motion.
Finished?
Paul shifts feet again.
Cloth has a different motion this time,
sliding off and bending upward,
like a set of wings.
The kid sits back on his heels,
reptile-still.
Paul takes out five $1 bills.

Careerist's Reading

At the center
of a small group, after the reading,
my boyfriend's getting worked up, driving
home his point, unaware of their stares,
my discomfort.
He is like a folding chair
I cannot close,
a shutter banging in the wind,
cup of red wine
jumping up and down in
his hand as if it were
his beating heart he held there.
I look down at my feet,
stare at the white
gallery walls
as he derides careerists
and career envy.
The wine has opened a vein
and his pain pours out.
Someone he knows from AA
has dropped his crackers on the floor.
My boyfriend grinds them to powder.

Red Snappers

Whatever fish were,
I did not know these
mottled red/gray
spray-painted tubes
nose-down in the bucket.
My five-year-old hand
grabbed a tail; its slipperiness
anchored it.
My grandfather and his
mariner friends
let out loud guffaws
at my first encounter
with the unfairness of weight.

At the Slot-Car Races

Tiny hunks of metal
flinging themselves around a donut
just duck your head and push forward
flip out
land
upside down.
What prizes?
the short attention span
the churning glory
smiles congealed
flashbulb lightning and
spattered gravel
the dust of the rec-room
in your throat
another minuscule wipeout
miniature mortality.
At least in Brian's basement
there's fake sagebrush
a locomotive town whose inhabitants' lives
change every eight seconds.
What a comfort to be able to bring it about so regularly,
And at least in Brian's basement
there's no dents in the particleboard paneling
from where the slot cars
in their tragic, limited cheapness
tried, for once, to fly.

Dorothy's Poem

The passengers seem to be saying,
after all, why bother?
The little faces strewn with graffiti
stare at us from behind paper windows.
I loved the flowers that would drop from the bushes,
or the severed heads of dolls
that would pop up in unexpected places.
You see, I'm this little amputated person
walking around,
with no ancestral pictures on the wall to stare at.
My past is not black and white
nor sepia tone,
just a disembodied hand
scratching at the door in dreams.
I cannot see the face it belongs to,
can't match up voices with gestures.
Nothing fits: the joists swell,
the train's hot breath is on my skull.
Rules make no sense.
I leave all my messages unanswered.
When people ask,
I tell them that the train is my home:
hands wave me to my destination as the faces
blur and spin faster.

Karl, Esther, Mark

I smoke. I smoke because it's all I know.
Years ago, ashes began my father —
he had no roots to speak of.
His foster family cared for him well enough
on the farm, the dry summers of central Michigan
cracking to brittle leaf.

The ashtrays in Karl and Esther's living room
always empty, and emptied;
ash-blue walls,
shelves filled with tasteful, hateful
bric-a-brac.

It was wonderful, my first cigarette —
at college, gin and tonic in the other hand
under the green dorm party light,
I felt like myself as never before,
a new grace descending
as I inhaled the autumn smoke
of those dried leaves.
Abroad, I studied the exotic labels
on the packs: filigreed lettering,
Mongols on horseback.

All our relations
agree to disagree:
we shrink from each other
in mutual distaste
at the obligatory gatherings,
even as we smile and
extend a papery hand.

Esther does not smoke.
(She merely appears as a puff, a cloud,
wan face and powdery hair,
nervous, thin hands plucking at her
apron, hoping aloud that the pork chops are
not too dry.)
Karl does, with a brandy preferably,
but he prefers that I don't.
I have to sneak out of the house to do it,
like some shameful act;
my friend hides them for me in her
glove compartment
until I move away.

Now I'm the nomad on horseback,
scattering Karl and Esther's ashes over London:
they dribble from the end of my
neglected cigarette.

New Name
for Mom

"Lisa," I tell her, at age 6.
"I want to be called Lisa from now on."
So she does. But there is a tiny
mocking pause before each utterance of the name:
"Would you like a glass of milk ... Lisa?"
"Are you going outside now ... Lisa?"
With her patient compliance, my mother
is teaching me how to be myself, how to
be at peace with the name and self
I was born with — not an easy lesson.
As the afternoon wears on, my new name
begins to feel more uncomfortable.
(It's like the time
I had my hair permed for a wedding.
It looked so odd it made me cry.)
Mom gives me time to chafe at the name
that has begun to rub spots on my psyche
raw. She doesn't quit
until I tell her to abandon it.

Slacker's Rant

I'm like,
angst-ridden, y'know?
The 7-Eleven glares green & red
against the hazy night sky.
It's a fine night for a holdup
and the parking lot looks mean.
Inside I search for the Big Gulp's
energy suck,
scrounge in the public microwave for crusts
of fossilized burrito.
The dirty soles of my feet
sob with unmet needs.
The frozen food case hisses,
"There is no escape."
Yeah, it's a fine night
For being held up.

Acknowledgments

"Adolescence": French translation published in *L.P.D.A.* in the USA. English version published in *Dreamscapes* (Spiral Stairway Press, no. 1, Spring 2009)

"To a Young Swimmer" and "Ice Skating": *Evergreen Review* #113

"Careerist's Reading" and "Dorothy's Poem": *Dreamscapes* (Spiral Stairway Press, no. 1, Spring 2009)

"Red Snappers": *The Outlaw Bible of American Poetry* (Thunder's Mouth Press, 1999)

"At the Slot-Car Races": *The Unbearables Assembling Magazine*

"Karl, Esther, Mark": *Long Shot*, vol. 14

ABOUT THE TYPE

One of six typefaces created in conjunction with Microsoft's ClearType text-rendering technology (and the initial letter "C"), Constantia, released in 1983, takes its name from Latin, meaning "constancy." At odds with company lawyers whose fear of trademark infringement continued to narrow the choices of possible nomenclature, its designer John Hudson, one evening, singing psalms during vespers, heard "constantia" intoned. He later confessed to the sight of seabirds prompting his regret that he had not chosen to call the typeface Cormorant.

* 9 780981 767871 *